RANGE LIGHT

Range Light

Author photo: Peter Mathew
Cover image: Louise Oxley
Cover design: Ralph Wessman

ISBN 9781763653047

Walleah Press
South Launceston
Tasmania, Australia 7249

www.walleahpress.com.au
ralph.wessman@walleahpress.com.au

RANGE LIGHT

Louise Oxley

About the author

Range Light is Louise Oxley's third collection of poems. Her first, *Compound Eye*, was commended in the Anne Elder Award for a first book of poetry, and her second, *Buoyancy*, was shortlisted in the WA Premier's Literary Awards. Louise has won major national awards, among them the Bruce Dawe (twice), Melbourne Poets Union and Tom Collins prizes. Her poems have been anthologised in several Best Australian volumes, *Contemporary Australian Poetry* (Puncher and Wattmann) and *Contemporary Australian Poetry in Chinese Translation* (John Kinsella and Ouyang Yu, eds.). A selection of her work, *Sitting with Cézanne*, is Picaro Press's *Wagtail 41*. Louise lives and works in Lutruwita/Tasmania.

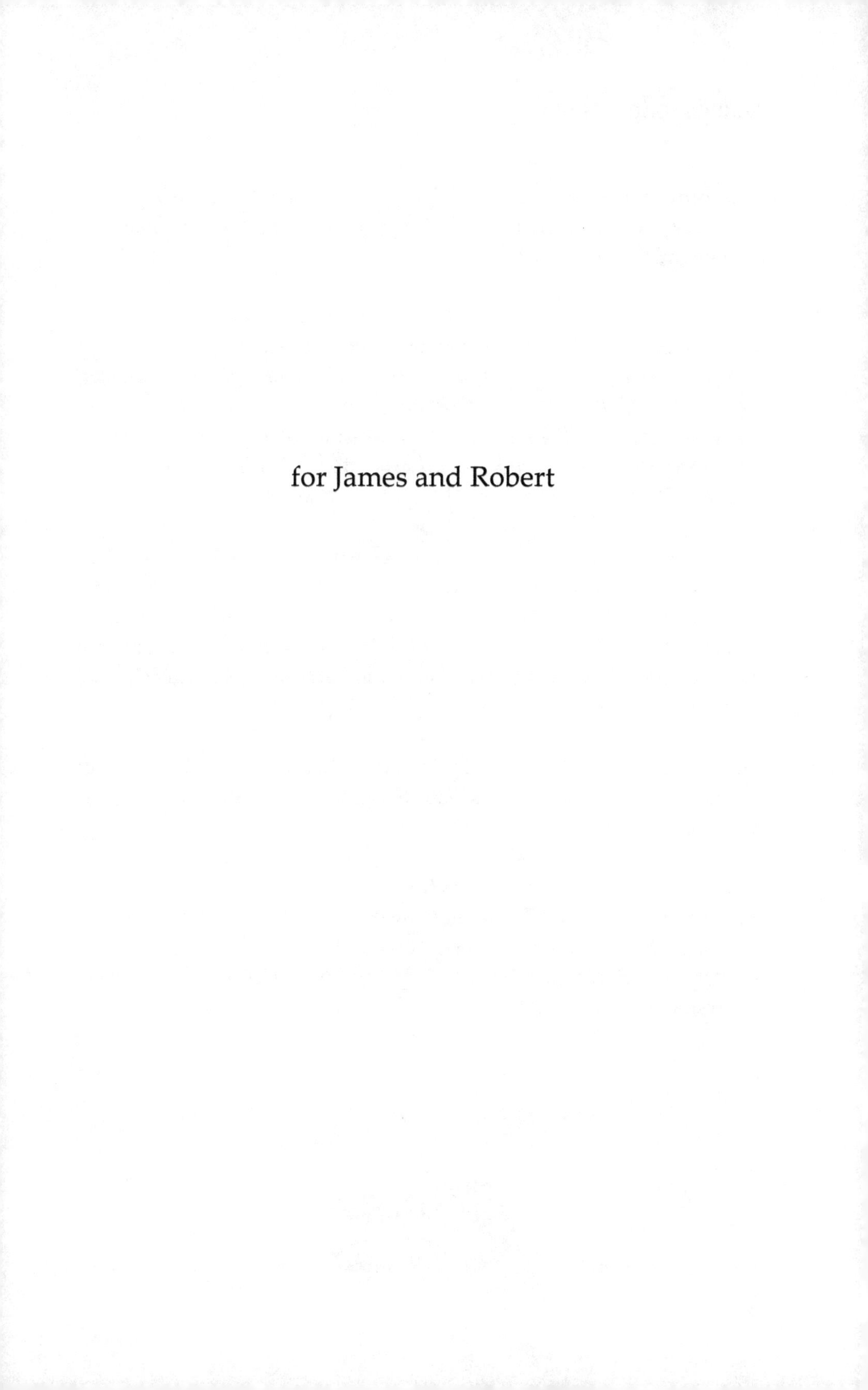

for James and Robert

Acknowledgements

This project has been assisted by Arts Tasmania and also by the Australian Government through Creative Australia, its principal arts investment and advisory body.

I am grateful to the editors of the publications in which some of these poems first appeared: *Arc Magazine* (Canada), *Australian Book Review, Australian Poetry Anthology Vol.11, Australian Poetry Journal, Birdsong: a Celebration of Bruny Island Birds, Blue Giraffe, Canberra Times, Cordite Poetry Review, Island, The Night Road* (Newcastle Poetry Prize anthology), *Punchbowl Poets and Painters, Quicksilver Water* (anthology of Oasis Women's Poetry), *Rochford Street Review* and *StylusLit*.

A number of poems in this collection were written for two Bett Gallery Poets and Painters projects. For the second of these, the Big Punchbowl Project, the Gallery partnered with the Tasmanian Land Conservancy. Thank you to all involved in these projects for the creative opportunity they provide, and to my generous collaborators, Troy Ruffels and Thornton Walker.

Thank you also to Kristen Lang for her leadership of the More Than Human Poetry Project, for which 'Seedling' and 'Soft rain for days' were created.

Thanks are also due to TasWriters (formerly Tasmanian Writers Centre), the Hobart City Council and the University of Prince Edward Island, Canada (UPEI) for a writer's residency at UPEI in 2011. 'Range Light', 'Invitation to Earnscliffe' and 'The Corvids' were written as a result of this residency.

CONTENTS

4. after Brett Whiteley   45

5. Stone of Return   53

Notes and Attributions   66

1. Range Light

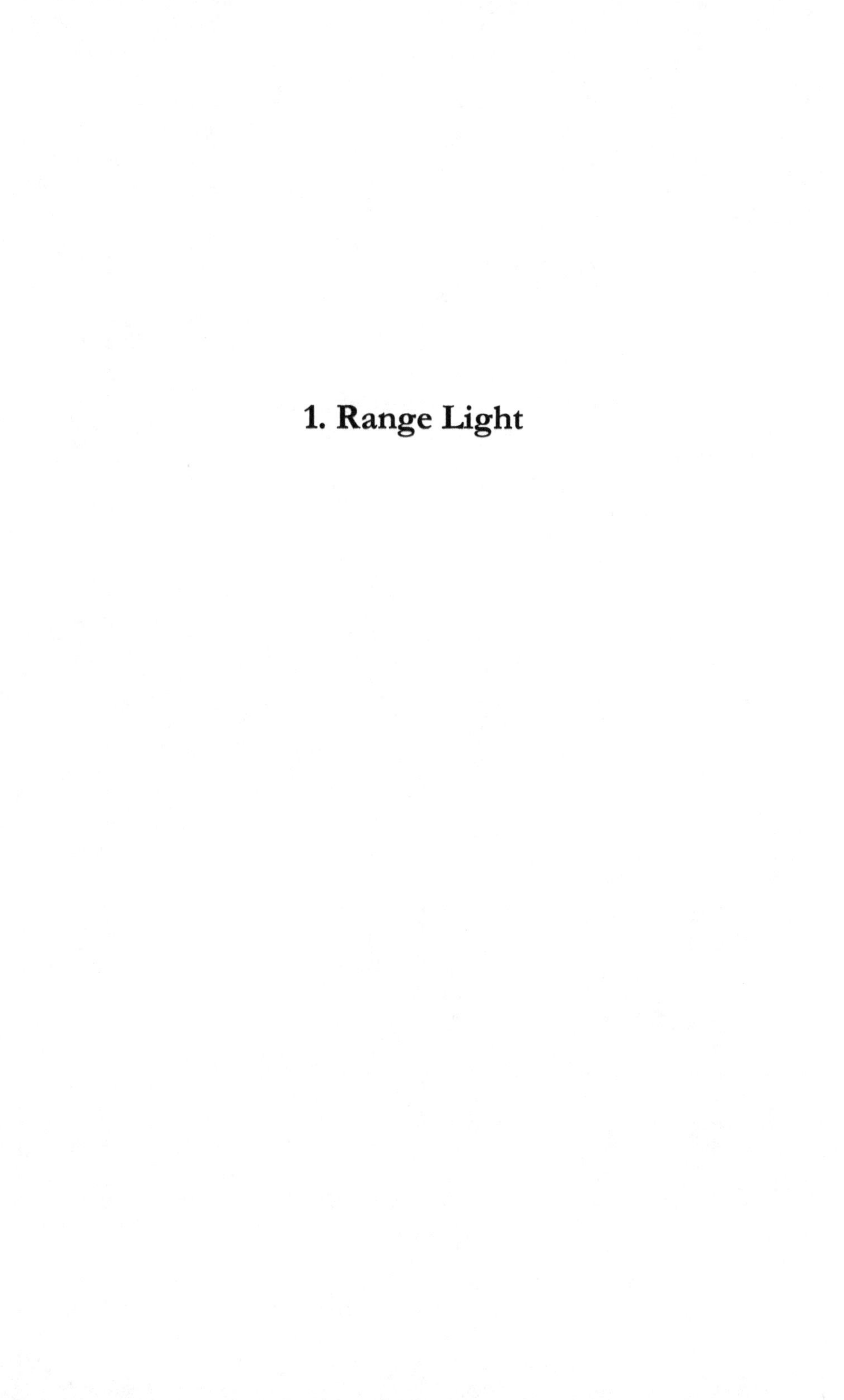

Orbit

Orbit: a rut made by a wheel. To go
forwards or backwards, the wheel must turn.

Forwards, not backwards, is the way you think
you want to go. High overhead, three eagles

circle. You want to go with them, eagle
parents and young, take the path they take.

The path: child around mother, moon around earth.
It's a matter of gravity; eagles

feel gravity in their feathers. They read
turbulence, the true shape of clouds, understand

lift and bank, know the shape of their own wings.
One day the mother's gone. But watch and wait.

Watch the sky and wait. Remember, you can want
to go back, to see her again. The wheel must turn.

Self-portrait with oars

It's good to go backwards,
the sky sliding over your face
like a loved hand;
if you tilt your head to the sun
and close your eyes
it doesn't matter at all
(so long as you're in open water
and it's calm).

I tried it yesterday.
I braced my feet and leaned
back with the pull –
tsha-*glop* click, tsha-*glop* click –
again and again,
ripples pattering under the bow
and the sun illuminating
the blood in my eyelids.

When I opened my eyes,
rapt as a mystic,
I had gone full circle.
I'm told that in Aymara
the past is in front of you;
it's what you can see.
The tricky future creeps up behind
and takes you by surprise.

I took this photo of my shadow
yesterday morning, early.
I'm about to enter the sea
and go round and round by mistake.

Invitation to Earnscliffe

for Libby Oughton

There are no hills;
but for a slight inflection beyond the road,
where one maple inflames the birchwood,
the land runs grazed and flat to the sea.
As you make your turns, left and left,
a squirrel streams across the road like a ribbon.
If you walk to the end of the road, you'll have sea on three sides.
Keep going, and the dog-rose will slow you, the sedge
give ground to you. Back up the road
you'll have passed a herd of Ayrshires
settled over their foldaway legs. Number 1546
is the curious one. She'll heave herself up,
horns raised like a pitchfork, and sway to the fence
to raise her slimy nose to you, the tip of a grey tongue
entering one nostril, then the other,
her eye-whites like old moons. As it's Fall,
the farmer will be out in the drizzle making silage,
his four straight silos capped like schoolboys,
his machines rumbling in mud the colour of drying blood.
If you turn right after the farm, you'll reach the beach.
There you can gather dulse. Roasted, it will welcome strangers.
At low tide, check the sandspit for harbour seals;
in the lee of rock, inflating shadows.
The house at Earnscliffe was dragged across the ice by oxen
and set down beside the flat road. In the afternoon
a blue jay – racing cyclist! – veers out of the spruce
for a biscuit, which he hammers at until it breaks.
In the morning, seagulls are over the fields
like pockets of early snow; a swarm of starlings
twists away like smoke.
When you wake at Earnscliffe you turn to see wind
herding rainclouds out to sea, leaving surprised mouths of blue.
A school of fish in the shower curtain passes the window
in currents of cloud. By the bed is a Hudson's Bay rug,

to remind you, every day when you stand,
how the Hopi were robbed.
If you're lucky at Earnscliffe, a skunk,
Lowell's fearless alien, will insinuate her pungent tail
through the mudroom door.
Each window has a curtain of a different length and colour.
Over the sofa is a rug so light and warm
you'll want to sit in the rocking chair and take up needles,
and from the ceiling, the diagonal length of the room,
hangs the son's organic kayak, hand-smoothed to solid honey,
its mute prow nosing the far corner. Beneath it
you will move like water.
The kitchen at Earnscliffe has much to nourish you:
beach-combings, an Inuit game of chance for hunting walrus,
Chinese lanterns bright as winter oranges,
geraniums propagating on the wood-box.
The kettle bounces marbles on the iron stove
to tell you the water's ready for tea, the fire-box
crammed with birch and the flue melodious as a throat-singer.
This is when geese make ready to leave, fluid arrowheads
against a sky that catches fire each evening and burns sideways,
a square reflected by the happy angle of windows
on the opposite side of the house.
And at your shoulder, a framed embroidery that reads
Think Spring in wobbly script.

Heifers

They suit this life and live it so completely.
At trough or creek-bed, under pine or eucalypt,
belly high in club-rush or milk-thistle,
they embody beastly carelessness. Or, to be
more fair, their enthusiasm's shared.
They gather and settle in any shade, diorama-still.
Sometimes a head swings to a flank,
sometimes a tail. Then one unlocks and bends her knees
and lets the back end follow, now
a mound of loam with moving parts.

Belonging comes easily to them. They stand
at licking distance, their bluish muscular tongues
rough, rhythmical, neighbourly.
See their slow, purposeful line to the waterhole,
tails dangling like loose rope. Let them slosh
and wallow, sink their clawed hooves into clay,
stare as wood-ducks clatter up
or the cormorant return.

If they had a vocabulary, finesse
wouldn't be in it. They trample the freshest hay,
belching their grassy breath (a quick croak in the throat)
and, holus bolus, bring the lot back up
to chew their circular chew again.
Dung pipes out of them like failed brioche
and when their season comes, they mount each other
without fuss. Rollicking down the fenceline
they stop day-trippers in Subarus, charm
women walking terriers. Bless their shamelessness,
their mastery of the steady gaze.

Aftertaste

Eating was at the heart of it; their love was alimentary.
It was linguine, creamy and tangled.

They rolled salt olives on their tongues and spat the pits
at careless angles where they pinged and hissed
against the fire. They pursed and stretched their lips
to say *bruschetta* as instructed by the earnest guide
on one of their imaginary Italian trips.

Over her upturned mouth he dangled
slippy oysters, scarlet capsicum in blistered strips.
Sardines she lusciously butterflied.
By candlelight they put the world to rights,
sighing over twice-cooked pan-fried duck. Yes, this

was us: wholesome, wholehearted. Now we feast
together only in the mind. But in the mind, at least.

Riding out

for Bec

Sunday afternoons we ride, if you can get away.
Often we follow the creek – determined water
hitting stones, hitting stones – then scramble uphill,
dislodging moss, ducking whips of prickly melaleuca,
and stop to watch for eagles, dizzying ourselves
with looking up, like children on a swing.
We aim to ride a circuit,
not to return the way we came.

Comfort is in our old knowledge:
our past that demands to be left undisturbed,
the four-beat hoof-fall on the gravel, the clash of stirrups
when the mares walk close – a dapple grey
and red sabino the colour of Sinai sand.
We talk of the Arabians of Lady Blunt,
bargainer with Bedouin,
and dream of trekking to the Pyramids.
Nearing sixty, we need to make it happen soon.

A yellow-topped post is where our paths diverge.
A goodbye hug's precarious. The ground is rough;
the horses shift and swing, sensing home.
I scan the hills for words. You're returning to a house
that's all but empty, where the man you chose for kindness
will be where you left him by the window,
in his recliner, staring out. Around us,
peppermint gums hang limp and bluish in still air.
Their trunks, as smooth as human skin,
have creased somehow, in growing.

Round Trip

Alonnah to Lunawanna, Bruny Island

At the homestead, pumpkins reach through wallaby wire
to settle lengthwise, flower and fruit outside the boundary.

From here the road's unsealed and rough. Jolted, shaken
from the steering wheel, drivers lift their hands.

A shadow on the gravel verge becomes a green rosella, its limp head
turned away, a stiffening blue-shot shoulder slightly raised.

Farther on, the early farms are still announced by English oaks
at driveway gates or single pear tree in a sheep-worn field,

but most have been repurposed, selling Premium Produce:
oysters, honey, cheese. They've brought the saleyards home.

Incursion leaves its other signs: too-green Spanish heath, armed
thistle volunteers – the seed escaping still, blackberries shrinking

from the orange dust that spits up off the road that bends to meet
the Channel and a remnant cemetery among the pines and casuarinas.

The headstones here are mostly worn to silence, though some
with grander names have been restored: *Troman Ezekiel, Bolton Stafford Bird.*

Hannah Green, 4 months can be deciphered with the help of fingertips,
18 seventy-something. May she rest in peace. But this would seem unlikely;

from somewhere in the backyard pile of rusting cars and water tanks
next door, Johnny Mathis heartbreak songs appropriate the air.

Below, where long sheer breakers flip, replace each other and withdraw,
a delicate wrack-line forms of seaweed beaded like a string of capers,

and another kind that's garnet-red and tasselled. A fluoro tennis ball
and length of yachting rope unravelling at both ends

have made their way into my hand. The sky's an open, dizzying blue
and seems still, but everything, as ever, is in motion. The one

cloud stretches, dropping bits; becomes a fancy chicken
trailing tatty pantaloons, as Hannah might have, had she lived.

A For Sale sign's appeared outside the homestead sheds: *Your chance for boutique
farmstay or new eco-home*, where sheep once clattered in for shearing

and onions hung to dry. For now, the brazen pumpkins fruit, three
cabbage moths twist up and up, the green rosella must be taken off the road.

Listening for the road

A rush of wind through the big radiata
sounds like your Renault on the gravel,
like you returning, calmer,
clouds of spent anger settling behind you.
It sounds like you driving down the hill
towards the house where I sit in late sun
with wine and poems on the garden bench
we assembled only yesterday,
looking up to the road from time to time,
to the massive pine, its needles seething,
its branches swaying like resolve,
between gusts going quiet.
Wrens fan out across the grass
like a search party. The sea breeze goes on
entering the tree and leaving it,
which is the sound of you
not rounding the gravel bends, not coming.

The Bat Corridor

Or we could leave the house, the pressure
of its walls and light, its hard words
bumbling against the windows,
and go down to the gully where the creek-bank
collapses with the autumn rains, something
you could fall for and put your lips to.
Come on, bring the mattock for the thistles;
hold it between us if you wish.

We won't know what makes them
unwrap the bandaged thumbs of their bodies
and bear away from the canopy
the moment the day's balance tips towards night;
we won't decipher their insect-seeking sonar,
or tally the number of beetles they catch
and the number they miss.
Yet these little crepuscular bats,
flying by hand, led by their petalled noses,
have us mesmerised in the spiky pea,
motionless, transported.

Scouts sent ahead of the night, detachments
from dark like escaped pocket linings,
one is suddenly there, a sharp dip and yaw
over the paddock, then gone; there
and gone, a relay of presence and absence.
They are mystery and guesswork;
their flickering fly-past in the half-light is enough
to make us question the worth of seeing clearly
and settle for partial blindness; enough,
when it's time to go in, to make you
shift the mattock to the other hand.

Graces Road

Rise above it, my mother used to say,
and now she's old, she herself is something I must rise above.
Just now, to separate myself, I turned and drove,
and finding Graces Road, followed its name
upwards to paddocks that a summer of scant rain
had worked into yellow and mauve.
Someone who had loved
this arc of land had turned things so its hay
could harvest the sun, and – who knows? – maybe
without forethought had named its road with a word
that drew me up like first light from grey
to yellow, then caught me in the whole half
circle of the day and removed
me, the dark hills around me like a sleeping herd.

Casket

From her armchair by the fire
where she sits all day most days,
she tells me the box has been delivered,
and could I fetch it from the hall.
With its clean partition
it might have been designed to house
a chess set's felled opponents – black
in one half, white in the other – except
that its dimensions are the undertaker's,
and for now only my father's half
will be occupied.
                    Viewed from the side
the grain in the pine makes a desert scene,
dunes backing away and away.
It gleams, somehow, from within,
like sun through a settling sandstorm
or honey held up to the light.
My mother's eyes are steady when she says
when her turn comes
she's perfectly happy to be put inside.
She wants to have somewhere to go
and to know where she's going.

Range Light

after Kim Morgan's *Range Light, Borden-Carleton, PEI* (2010)

'though each thing dies into its own becoming'
John Burnside

Suppose there were souls,
and they could leave one body
to inhabit another;

suppose body could mean
not only flesh sheathed in skin
or scales or carapace,
but any construction
– brick or stone,
weatherboard or shingle –
so long as it's lit from within;

and suppose that, by reason of
its one seaward window
where burners and reflectors were set,
its beacon going out after dark
to ferrymen crossing the strait,
this little lighthouse, one of a pair
that aligned like good parents
to guarantee safe passage,
could die when it was of no further use,
and its soul would leave it then.

Suppose an artist, out walking
high on a cape
overlooking the new bridge
of steel and concrete,
came across the lighthouse
alone now, useless,
blank as a snowman,
and understood
that its soul was leaving.

Suppose the soul shadowed her
until one morning
she woke up knowing
she had to offer the lighthouse
the gift of safe passage
into its own becoming,
that she would fabricate a skin
for it to shed,
a skin of latex and mosquito netting
she would smooth lovingly
over the whole squat body
and peel off,

a skin that would make visible
its former life,
outside and inside at the same time,
its texture of cracked shingle
imprinted with the lost
labour of ice-boat men
hauling travellers across the ice,
with graffiti and flakes of paint,
with the laughter of ferry passengers
crossing to the Island
for Thanksgiving.

Suppose now that the artist
sews together the shed skin
and suspends this soft architecture
from the ceiling of galleries
across the country,
sending it out to bring it home,
that it hangs,
light-filled and toppling,
an almost-resurrection,
its past a haunting,
like a dream you can neither forget
nor clearly remember.

2. The Observatory Shore

The Observatory Shore

after *The Voyage in Search of La Pérouse* by Labillardière, May 1792

i. kangourou

Trailing orange legs, two rain-grey birds
part from the rain-grey sea, lift off and circle low,
waiting for us to be done. But we are slow
on eau-de-vie and cheese, giddy with the search
for stars, the unsteadying voyage. Citizen Riche
is squatting where a rivulet, stained brown
with fallen trees, lets in saltwater at its mouth.
When he steadies himself on his heels, beached
cockles crack and shatter; behind him, along the shore,
domed crabs, the bluish-violet of the evening, draw
in their delicate legs and upend themselves, turning
into sand. Riche sinks too. His lungs are burning.
Quietly he coughs. Blood spits on to his shoe,
the broken shells, the tracks of *kangourou*.

He's far advanced; he won't survive the voyage
and this far south, at forty-four degrees
in May, the winds that rise up from the seas
set fire to his chest. Mostly he avoids us,
keeps apart; he's curious in both its senses, dressed
in leather hat and gaiters, a gun, a shooter's sack,
cutlass, linen-padded forceps, and a sail-cloth vest
devised for specimens, with pockets front and back.
He's seeing, always, what is different from the known.
I watch him concentrated, hunched, alone
examining the tracks of *kangourou*, all his zeal
for science, not himself. He considers claw and heel,
the balancing tail, the resting forepaws' shape and splay
before their imprints and our own are washed away.

ii. cigne

Yesterday one of us shot, in flight,
a singular bird in the form of a swan,
as black as ours are white.
Its plumage shone.

A singular bird in the form of a swan,
its mate called from across the lake.
The plumage shone.
We have our research to do. We take.

Its mate called from across the lake,
the red beak wide, the neck a question.
We have our research to do. I undertake
to make a just description.

The red beak wide, the neck a question,
the shot bird held white feathers in its wing;
to make a just description,
precisely six. Only by killing

the bird that held white feathers in its wing
could we count and name this beauty:
precisely six. Only by killing
could we see the band at the beak's extremity,

could we count and name this beauty:
the eye's hard red, the grey amphibious feet,
the white band at the beak's extremity,
the swan black as the fire-hollowed trees

we found, the fire-blackened earth,
as black as ours are white.
To name and to describe its worth,
one of us shot a singular bird in flight.

iii. iridée

diplarrena moraea

No sooner do I pluck them
than they wither.
Pure and brief,

white as breakers,
as the inescapable salt,
white as thirst,

as perfectly bent
to their curve
as the cockles we find

everywhere stranded.
Three petals – three cheeks
and three more:

a palate and two
poking yellow tongues
with a spit of ink,

a gargoyle *enfantin*
or curious creature
lending its ears

to the laden gossip of bees.
White as linen
laid out for embroidery

or embroidery itself;
a new exotic stitch, perhaps,
for Alençon,

a thread-seller's dream.
Roused sleepers,
one furled bud

follows another out
into the light,
as if, *maman,*

your scissors, set down
for an idle moment,
stood up and blossomed.

Naming them is easy –
a name each for the old world
and the new,

yet I cannot keep them.
No sooner do I pluck them
than they wither.

iv. tempête

All night for nights, impetuous squalls.
Beneath the great mast we start a fire burning
to warn the *Esperance* we're casting anchor, pay
out our cable, unrig the main topgallant sail and wait
for rain along the dark horizon-line to clear.
Every word we speak is turned away and falls

into the sea, to the greyish shell-mixed mud, falls
foreign and unheard. There's nothing to hear but squalls
groaning in the timbers. We want a clear
view of what we've come to, not this black burning
in the throat and ears, this blind watch. We wait
to see the strait we've entered, its hills and inlets, pay

out our patience: no science for days. We're paying
dearly for this voyage. The good wine gone, men fall
into delirium or stupor, swigging brandy. They wait
for racing air to slow, for cloud to leave, for squalls
to die. No stars. Without their scattered burning,
without astronomy, we cannot know, it's clear,

what has become of us, so far from the clear
comfort of a length of street, where we simply pay
for what we lack, streetlamps lit each dusk and burning,
towns walled and warm, the pale slant of rain falling
quietly on cobblestones. Here it's *à l'envers* – autumn squalls
in May, the winds we need to drive us make us wait

and then torment us with the scent of oyster flesh. The wait
for flesh – woman, fish or fruit – is carried clearly
in the eyes of every man, in every voice. We're squalling
gulls above a shoal, stalled and buffeted. We try to pay
no mind but little mind remains; we concentrate on detail: the fall
of the barometer, the height of wave or tide, the burning

that erupts around the ship, the drowned burning
of phosphorescent stars, ghosts that wait
an agitated moment in the waves before they fall
back and are gone. Still, my task's to make a true, clear
account of Nature's phenomena, no matter the price to be paid,
even while enduring them; even these South Sea squalls

will repay us with knowledge, though the long wait
burns us now, and we'll investigate, when the squalls clear,
whatever should meet us, wherever the eye falls.

3. Time on the Reserve

Bones at Barney Ward's Lagoon

It lies as if arranged there for a totem:
a few steps back from the lagoon's black mud
and white as east coast sand, a skeleton.

It's lost all flesh. A raven, Devil or some
other worshipper has taken the muscle and blood.
It lies as if arranged there for a totem

at empty, delicate angles – jawbone, pelvis, sternum,
a coronet of vertebrae around the skull – odd
remnants, white as east coast sand. The skeleton's

a wallaby dismantled, a solemn
re-patterning of bone; loss in scrambled code.
It lies as if arranged there for a totem,

unfleshed, unfurred, uncoupled; emblem
of life's underpinnings laid out.
White as east coast sand, a skeleton.

Two saplings – black wattle trees – grow over them,
these bones; silver-green and coming into bud.
It lies as if arranged there for a totem:
white as east coast sand, a skeleton.

Time on the Reserve

i.
the zoologist speaks —
between my boots a scorpion
moves unheard

on the tendril
of a blue love-creeper
a resting wasp

a line of ants
to the ancient grasstree —
distant smoke

ii.
in a new lagoon
the plink of banjo frogs
ten years silent

water-ribbons
flattened by the flood
raise flower spikes

by still pools
the last shotgun cartridge
sky blue

iii.
two saplings
over scattered bones —
timekeepers

pink orchid
in cubes of wombat dung –
an outstretched hand

smooth fungus
crowning leaf litter –
our shadows pass

To be lizard

to wait in a crevice
      for moths to end
         their fluttering silvery fall

turned thinly sideways
      still   cold   silent
         ready with a dark tongue

outside language
      nothing but a faint
         pulse in the ears

minus a tail
      on the chancy road to freedom
         and not a backward glance

or sun-flattened:
      the wishful thinking
         of warm rock

On Solitude

*

Rousseau

He wants to know what he is. Now
that he feels a foreigner at home, *lurching
from fault to fault and error to error,*
he writes out his disgrace.
He divides the little island into squares,
visits each in every season,
takes his magnifying glass to box and balsam,
notes the self-heal's forking stamens
and, ankle-deep in thyme and clover,
sends to Neuchâtel for rabbits.
He fills his room with grasses, moss and lichen,
lies back in the rowboat and drifts across the lake.
It's last light when he turns for home,
drawn by water shirring over shingles.
He knows he won't return
to that fertile, lonely place, but
isn't it the same to dream that I am there?

*

Nietzsche

He wants to go beyond himself; so far
that he can look down on the stars.
He's *an arrow of longing* for the final summit.
He steps up mountainsides
and down again, meeting with nobody,
listening to the trees, the streams,
the simmering springs, the wings of tender birds;
listening for so long that now he speaks
only the mountain-climber's tongue –
his mouth is for his ears, and his alone.
Before he set out, he had wished to see
the ground and background of all things,
to be faithful to earth,
but his foot is the wanderer's foot,
extinguishing the path behind him.

*

Emerson

He wants to be a man again. He leaves
his books, his room, *the din and craft of the street,*
and enters the sea's hush.
He stands where the earth is a shore
and looks across its silence.
The eye demands a horizon; he will never be tired
so long as he sees far enough.
A slender bar of cloud
slides through the sky like a fish;
a sandspit lifts from the sea and hovers.
The air has *so much life and sweetness*
it will be painful to return indoors.
A tree, rimed with light at the water's edge,
shows him that light is the first painter,
and that the artist or poet might set the tree
afloat, aloof, making of its *kindred impressions —*
acorn, pine-cone, butterfly, bivalve, flame or bud —
one blue touchstone for the senses,
mute music singing
nothing can befall me that nature cannot repair.

Blue Halo

after Charles Blackman's *They brought her ribbons of yellow and crimson and great clusters of flowers* (c. 1980)

He paints the flowers she brought him on his breakfast tray
the day she called the marriage off, and returns them to her, framed.
He knows her eyes have long ago resigned. He used to say
he had eyes enough for both of them, and read her Dostoyevsky.
She travels on a shaft of memory
to the question mark that she was born with, a cul-de-sac
of sightlessness, and comes to rest in flowerdrift. Landscapes
liquefy and vaporise; yellow and crimson ribbons fly. The petals' waxed
imperfect surfaces, tricking light, send out rings of blue, the shade
exactly that entices bees. Like her, they
don't need human eyes. Her fingers find their way
into the centre. And now she floats, held up by flowered hands.

Native Hens

And then, when autumn sun has steadied at the hilltop,
they stream into view like renewed hope; native hens –
the usual six – up the front paddock and on to the lawn,
emboldened now that the terrier,
old and slowing, has taken no chicks for years.

They peck and peck at invisible things in the grass,
their tails jerking like levers on some out-of-whack machine,
one gathering the clan: *check, check, check,*
before they all move on.

They do the comforting work of family chooks
without the fuss. I love the way they look
exactly alike, female and male,
with their oversized feet and redcurrant eyes,

their bodies like liquid slate, and the way
they scatter and regroup like drops of something molten,
holding together day and night, their rusty-saw calls
making light of the darkest hours.

Today though, something new – a loosening, letting go.
One lowers itself, breast to earth, and grazes while prone
like a goose, and another joins it, head to tail:
two wild and flightless creatures by a house,
less fearful than they were, and resting.

Soft rain for days

Rain so fine it doesn't fall, but hangs, a deep white
exhalation. It fills gullies, erases summits.

On the eastern slopes, houses disappear. Across the waterway
the flattened island is uncertain of itself, distance unclear.

The Channel has become a room with drawn curtains,
profoundly quiet, like a forest under a fresh snowfall.

Even the grunting ferry has lost its voice.
So many disappearances: blackwoods for powerlines,

leek-orchids under tarmac, the boobook's answer music
silenced by city lights. These small big things. And yesterday,

downed eagles: a breeding pair riddled with shot.
The swollen creek in its brown churning glory folds

back into itself, lifts over rock in frilled, trembling shelves.
Floes of white foam shudder in the cutbanks.

The sky lowers, the creek rises. For now. As if to comfort me.

Parachute

How like a flotilla of stalled parachutes is the canopy
of this lone eucalypt, caught and agitated by a morning squall.

Laden cumulus barge across the window,
a flow field breaking brightly open, only to close again.

Looks like the weather's heading south, might reach you
as you're moving out, extracting *yours* from *ours*. On your knees,

taping dusty boxes. That ripping sound, the ragged final tear.
You'll seal the cracks, only to open them again.

I know the contour of your back, the way you bite the tape,
the small and careful hands that smooth it down,

the way you'll squat to take the weight of things
you valued once, your merciless, thinning hair.

When I look up, the squall has passed, the tree returned to itself.
The canopy is nothing but a living mass of leaves; shroud lines

simply branches. Only the idea of the parachute remains: the terrifying
leap, the jolt that breaks the fall, the slow, exhilarating descent.

Tenure

The day I opened the letter, the sky was cloudless, the blue unbroken. That night I found my crumpled car in the back corner of a restaurant. The customers took it away piece by piece. I forgot to take photos for the insurance. Next thing I was in in surgery. They removed the wrong baby. Another night my mother was young again. It was her wedding day. I couldn't find a dress to wear. I stood at the open wardrobe pushing bent necks along the rail, one way and then the other. The empty clothes were a grandfather's dead weight: tobacco-brown tweed, corduroy. Finally I found a dress. My arms disobeyed, my body wouldn't go through the right holes. As soon as I got it on, my sisters appeared in identical dresses. The day I opened the letter, the blue called out, *remember, nothing is yours, even if he fights you for it:* not the comforting hills, not the tree-ferns that brighten the gullies, not the slaters minding their business under the woodpile. The blue insisted, *look through me, look again,* even at the tiger snake at your heel, coiled in its magnificent defence.

When she thinks of Robert Hass's aspens

Picture a woman told
she'd never manage the place on her own,
under an old shed lean-to on a spring evening.
Fillets of kindling shear away from her tomahawk
in thin, even strips. She sets herself a test –
how fine can she cut it? – simply for the pleasure
in knowing she will neither pass nor fail.
She straightens, softens her grip on the axe.
It swings and comes to rest against her leg,
almost companionable. These days
she can stop what she's doing
and stand in her dreams whenever she likes.
She can stand to attend, and not to attention.
The home-paddock stringybark is rustling
in an unsteady westerly. She listens to its *fsh, fsh, fsh,*
sees how it bends, how the loose leaf-clumps,
peppered with yellow-green buds,
sway and part, opening to make way.
On the lee side, the long leaves swivel and flicker,
fully, greenly alive. But where the wind first strikes,
the branches are brittle, leafless, greying,
as if on that side the tree's been bleeding out.
A slow poisoning, too little water or too much,
beetle galleries in the heartwood, old age?
She's not sure why. But she is sure
that this lopsided, mostly living thing
is something she can safely love.
When she thinks of Robert Hass's aspens,
how language cannot truly say what a tree does,
she knows she's returning to her right mind.

Then there's the question of what a tree feels.
Perhaps it's something like relief
to let those dead limbs go, to let them
crack and tear away, crash awkwardly
and break apart when the time comes,
which will be, she's learned,
when no-one's watching.

Towards Equinox

The end would have ended by now
– you're three years gone from here, after all –
        but for a bend in the road
                    the last before home
        where, catching the lowering sun
a guidepost blinks like a monitor,

like the evil eye, there each evening
                    over my shoulder
when I barrow hay to the horses
hoist hay nets, clip feed bins to the fence
                    check for injuries.
One fumble with a rug-strap
one nip from a carabiner
one misstep in the tying of a halter hitch
        – *your funny little bows* you called them –
                    and the eye is on me.

Front after front is storming the paddocks.
The slant force of wind
                its unforeseeable lulls and gusts
tears strips off trees, dismembers them.
A top-heavy white gum near the creek
                            loses its footing.
Roof-tin lifts and bangs
        like a demanding child.

It's as if, when all is arranged so that dark equals light
the cosmos designs experiments
        to test resistance
                strength of will.

Daffodils lie flattened, frilled noses in the turf.
It seems only right to rescue the fallen
stand them up again.

        Held in a vase
they imitate for a while their living selves
      even opening fat buds
           in a brief afterlife.

But space is what they need
         and being alone in it.
Out in the open where they're strongest
after the long light
        and the short
spring will come back for them
      its flashes of sun and storm
       rousing tatty heads
from winter burial.

Virescent, they're called. Greenish. Becoming green.

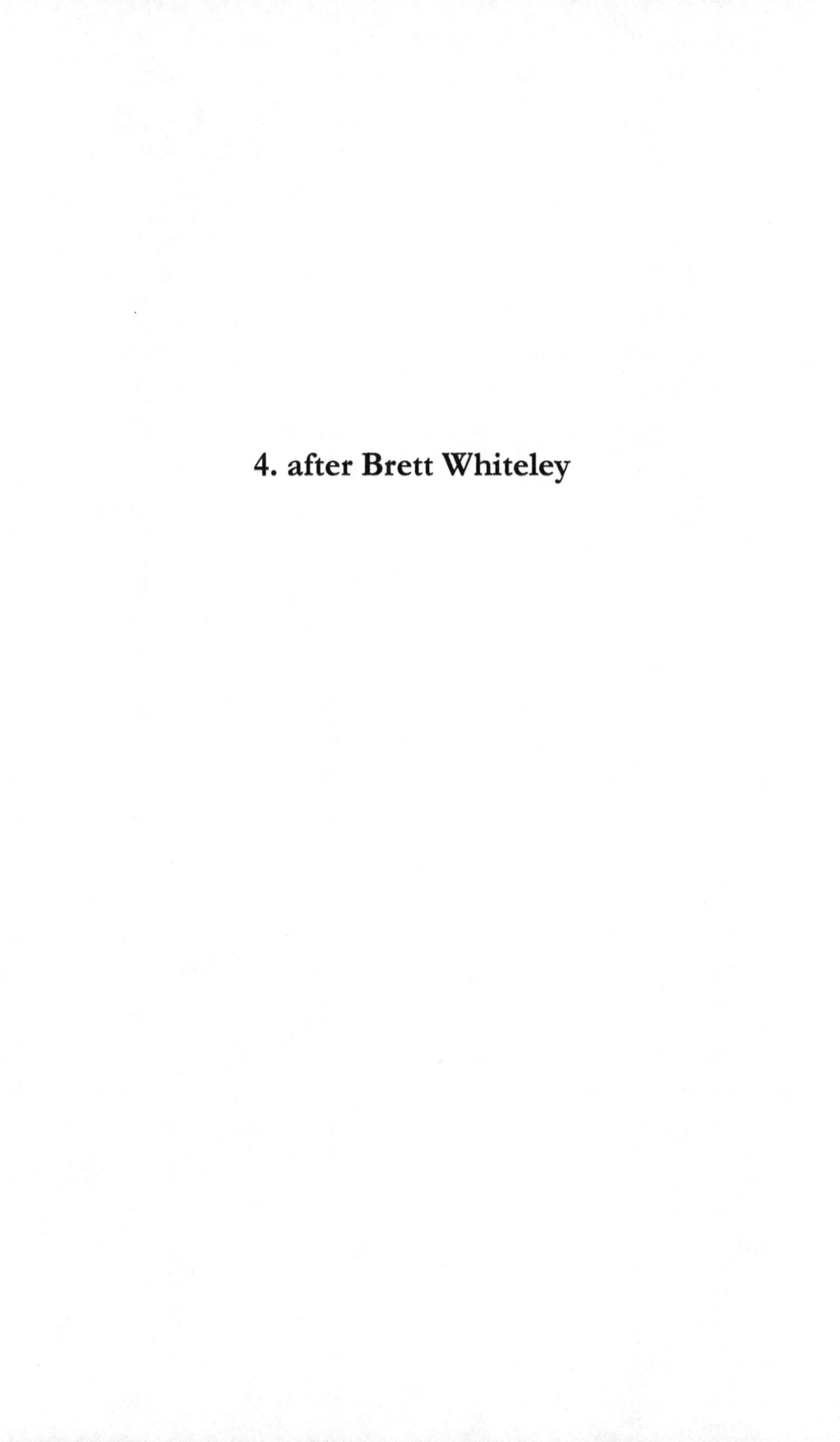

4. after Brett Whiteley

The Green Mountain (Fiji)

after the painting by Brett Whiteley (1969)

The skyward pitch of the hill in its green glory
rising heavy and indolent as the knee of a woman
sunbathing in a sarong,
and the thigh that leads from this knee,
an emerald downswelling syncline,
end where the womb's elastic triangle,
fronded and flowering, holds three
imperfectly white eggs,
expectant, fragile yet unbreakable
among a tumble of mellifluous treasures –
swollen sacs, pouches and bulges:
a ballooning Polynesian breast,
a giant scrotum of jackfruit,
an intestinal serpent –
all weighted with sunlight,
contented in their curvature
and insinuating themselves into paradise;
above this tumescent anatomy,
sent up from the nest like a dear wish
and stalled, a tracer hummingbird
peers down at the path she has taken,
as if to memorise its precise arc.
She will dart out and return
to warm her eggs again and again
or whirr away over the flank of Green Mountain
and be gone
at the bidding of the mind's eye.

Sensoreno

after *Sensoreno*, a portrait of his terrier, ink and collage on paper (1977)

Since everything's two-way, I've given Sense my eyes
and painted her in sumi-e. In ink, in present tense, we turn
and look, but don't quite meet your gaze. There's an animal

in all of us that cannot be relied upon, an animal
that trips us up or will not come to heel. The eyes
seem to say remorse. My hand moves over her; it knows the turn

of slumped spine, the haunch splayed out, and sweeps this turn
across the wall. To paint animal, first become animal.
We're masked. The point is not the mask, but what's behind it – eyes.

Or seeming eyes. We turn full circle twice, then sink to animal sleep.

Woman in Bath

after the painting by Brett Whiteley (1964)

There was fog on the windows,
inside and out.
She wound her hair into a bun
and eased into the shallow water.
I stood in the doorway, squinting.
                      I wanted her
curled into that ceramic curve
like an embryo in the shell.
I stood, squatted, paced about
and stood again at the door, deciding
what to give her and what to take away.
                The head I'd reduce
to a dented ellipse, tender as a crowning baby's.
Over the M of her raised knees I'd order an accident,
a blessing and violation: the showerhead
became a crescent moon that creamed
the wine-red cloth I'd placed between her legs;
                  behind her back
a pair of voyeur taps in housecoat blue.
I've captured something of the foetal bird
in the angle of the neck, a subdued alignment
of head and shoulder. Her breasts I figured
full and solid, a nipple hardening
beneath her arm.
              And for the limbs I thank
Modigliani: buttery dough rolled thin.
I could push them through my fingers.
She kicked out one cramped leg,
swung her haunches to the other side.

I got that right –
the movement she'd just made
and the one she'd yet to make. Later
I painted the living daylights out of the walls
till they were flat and still as the lake at Sigean.
She lifted her chin. *You still there, Brett?*
I'm freezing my tits off in here!
In art alone I could becalm us.

Reply from the Women of Tangier

after *The Majestic Hotel, Tangier (1967)*

So secretly together do we wear
our separateness, we're so complete
he gives us the white stare.

Easy to see decay and disrepair
in the spittle and hashish-ruined streets.
But secretly together we all wear

our place and time, our rightness here,
our journey from antiquity.
He gives us the white stare

and calls us names: the Olive Mafia.
We hold our desert gaze, defeat
his envy, and secretly together bare

our hennaed hands, our loosened hair,
our thighs for marriage rites, our feet.
He gives us the white stare,

but cannot penetrate the haze, can't bear
our vapour-of-midnight eyes, our heat.
So secretly together do we share
ourselves, he gives us the white stare.

5. Stone of Return

The Corvids

They're in from the overworked farms, the old
demolished slaughterhouses, the suburban tips.

We don't even need to look up; they find us,
like guilty memories – crows, ravens, jackdaws, rooks –
wherever we are on our small patch of concrete or earth.

One gives you the eye at your window, demanding
the meatballs you roll in your palm and leave on the sill;
one nests in your chimney, smoking you out.

We don't even need to look up; they recognise us.
Yet we go on pretending they all look the same,
like foreigners, don't seem to matter as much.

Even their voices are black, old bluesmen on repeat,
dolorous and comical at once. They talk over us,
never let up, on and on until dusk, when it's off

to the Charlottetown shore, up and down
from the Governor's trees like late-summer leaves
that can't make up their minds; a family of thousands

all having their say: the naggers, the meddlers, the histrionics.
Despite our scorn and our gas guns they're still here.
We don't even need to look up; they scold us, like hard truths.

Thistle Villanelle

'For we are conquerors and self-poisoners'
               Judith Wright

Taker of summers, paddock by paddock, it lies in wait
where trees were pushed aside, the country eaten bare.
Imagine if we'd cared. If Earth could have its say.

What can a thistle do but spread and settle? Arms raised,
ungraspable, it stakes a claim anywhere
it lands. Taker of summers, of paddocks, it lies in wait.

I jab and dig, heap pile on wilting pile till late,
pull thorns out with my teeth, sweat crawling in my hair.
Imagine if we'd cared. If Earth could have its say.

Each spike concealed in reeds or ditch will liberate
thousands upon thousands of pale and flimsy heirs.
Taker of summers, paddock by paddock, it lies in wait.

Some think they know. They tell me, *it can't penetrate
a pasture crop. Leave it alone.* I do not dare.
Imagine if we'd cared. If Earth could have its say.

And so, weedstock myself, I labour with mattock and spade
undoing indifference, re-doing penance and repair.
Taker of summers, paddock by paddock, it lies in wait.
Imagine if we'd cared. If Earth could have its say.

The Red Gurnard

Against an outgoing tide
he comes up sluggish and sideways
like a reluctant *No,*

breaks the surface
and spins under my arm,
his shocked skin flashing orange.

There is only unhinged mouthing
and raised hackles; his panic
is a slow internal bleed.

I know who he is:
shape-shifter from a life
with other rules for beauty,

for movement and sensation;
a wet and breathless life.
We're spellbound:

I only have eyes for his eyes,
black from the grottos,
his faltering fins,

his undersea sail in tatters,
his sequined sides,
his crown of spines.

Kiss me now, he says,
his argument perfectly formed.

Injury

For weeks a lump like a ball-bearing has lodged in my lower lip,
and a front tooth hangs on a hinge. I didn't see you coming;
no starlight or moon, just a blur of mist that lost itself in trees
and silenced the undergrowth. When you rushed the fodder bin,
hungry from winter-thin pasture, in that moment of collision,
woman with beast, in that lightning bolt of pain too sudden
for fear, I knew I would be changed. Up to my ankles in tarry mud,
I pushed my teeth in with my thumbs, leaned over, wobbled and bled.

Today, the shortest of the year, an easterly brings mist again.
The slaughterman sizes you up, grunts softly, goes back for a bigger gun.
I want to say this is coincidence, not revenge; or simply one thing
leading to another as it does when no-one stops to think.
I want to believe you won't see it coming, that you'll be living the good life
to the last: stepping forward for the next sweet tussock and the next.
Forgive me: I'm trying to reason you away. I keep my distance,
but the shot still reaches me in echo, sounding double.
I'm learning the new shape of my mouth with each pass of my tongue.

How to treat a dairy cow

Swap the number on her laser-printed electronic ear tag for a name.
Name her for something rare and precious, something
Earth has produced as a miracle. Emerald, say.
Name her without appropriation.

Consider her hourglass face. Her time hasn't been her own.
Give her time, cow time, a good twenty-five years.
Let her decide how she spends it.

Admire the yin-yang of her coat, her long, appraising stare,
her eyes that take in light and all she's seen, their secretive lashes.
Understand her blind spots.

Re-think your grammar: refuse *lactations* plural.
De-frenchify your lexicon. Lose the duplicity: if you eat it,
call it cow or calf, not beef or veal. Go further,

lose language altogether. Stand on all fours. Begin a day-long wait
on shit-slimed concrete to be hitched by your nipples to a machine.
Feel the stupefying cold make its way up through your legs,

between your hips, the skin slung between them like a collapsing tent,
and down your useless switchless tail, even as your full udder burns,
stretched and pendulous as a water-bomb, so swollen you have to straddle it.

Google udder size. You'll find her genes are engineered for yield
and milkability. Next, search markers for chronic stress, tie stalls, zero-grazing
systems. Don't trick her into thinking she's outside.
Ditch her virtual reality mask.

Look elsewhere. Follow Denmark's rulebook: install a tube-broom
scratcher and a salt-lick laced with molasses. She'll know exactly
what to do with them. Watching her, you may see something of yourself:
a need for trust, for unselfconscious pleasure.

Think Sikh. Judge the moral quality of the State by its cow protection laws.
Summon Khamadhenu, fragrant one, cow of miraculous powers,
cow that fulfils all desires.

Campaign for bovine rights. Persist. Feel for those who tell you
you know nothing about her. They're squeezed between the world
and their idea of the world. Let her keep a calf.

Or, if her last has just been taken, take the risk. Find her an orphan.
You'll be surprised how soon her eye-whites disappear,
her ears begin to slacken and hang backwards
as if they're starting to come loose.

Turn off the let-down music. She needs to hear only danger
and the bleating of her calf. Listen to her low lowing when he strays.
Learn to differentiate her calls.

If all that's too much to ask, do simply this: release her into pasture
with a tree to ruminate beneath and the company of her kind.
Expect nothing from her.

Now treat yourself. Go out on a cloudless night and stand
among the herd. Just you, stars, cows and the sound of tearing grass.

bird life sijo

*

Insects caught in corners bring a scarlet robin to my window.
Her fragile breast is sunrise to gentling dusk: a day in a bird.
She works alone, barely brushing the glass. So little divides us.

*

White cockatoos shout each other down through stringybarks,
tumbling like klick-clack toys. They tear everything to shreds: buds, fruit,
silence. Each head's a cache of knives. How can they pair for life?

*

A veil of rain on the hill. Hunched, tails dragging, native hens
see off intruders. The old pair bray in synchrony, as if one bird.
The family closes ranks and waits. They know their limits.

*

Ebb tide. Two oystercatchers fly to shore in steady parallel,
forage head to tail, shake their long toes free of grit. I fill a bag
with perished plastic, frayed rope, fishing line. I must not fail them.

Girl on a fencepost

It's been shared and shared:
a little girl of three, sitting on a fencepost,
singing to a horse.

Unrecognisable at first – sharp mostly,
thin and shrill – the melody resolves and settles
as she goes along,

perhaps because for her
it's the *singing to* that matters, not the song.
And yet what's come to her

is Heal the World.
To hear her running out of breath,
so that she doesn't quite articulate

the final consonants
of the refrain, is to hear again
the artless child in us we lose.

Bellowing cows upstage her
from the next-door paddock.
She ups the volume, sings above the din.

Her open palm moves up and down
between the horse's eyes,
a pressure the animal leans into.

It blinks more slowly. The eyelids
close and soften. The child's small fingers
come to rest around the bony nose

that could unseat her with the slightest push.
But no, the horse nods off,
the head dropping in little increments,

the tufted muscular lip twitching
in her lap in sleep. A second horse
standing by just out of frame

approaches now... She sees the pony coming, turns
and offers it that same small open hand,
her smile beneath the jammed-on hat

fearless, tender, as if
a better world were in her power.

Seedling

Then the first yellow flower forming on the seedling
catches the light like a Star of David pinned to a lapel,
and I see, hooked into the soil, the plastic arrow that announces,
as if a label makes it true, *Leb Mini Munch Cucumber,*
a sly belittling that it cannot counter or resist, this pale vine
whose forbear seeds might have left the Baanoub Valley
in the hands of a quiet man like my neighbour Kasim,
taken for safekeeping from his garden beside an olive grove,
its ancient trees tended through the ages by monks;
imagine militia threading the rows of split and twisted trunks,
Kasim running with nothing but a fistful of seeds
and the memorised layout of raised beds,
trellis lines and companion plantings,
approaching the coast and a slim chance of America,
seeds pressed to his chest like family secrets,
just as, further west, only six years ago, Nahla and Salem
brought rose seeds from Syria, hip pockets full and chafing
the legs of their twin babies, the seeds snatched from a plot
in a village beyond the mountains where birds no longer sing,
from songless village to desert camp to wheatfield
to the rosefield of their making in Beqaa,
a magenta sea of Damascus rose, thirty-petalled *sultani,*
honoured by Shakespeare and the Babylonians, buds gathered
at first light before the sun has emptied them of scent,
then stirred to a pink concoction perfected over centuries,
petals bleeding into boiling water for *mouneh* against the hardship of winter,
for syrupy *baklava, kanafeh, mehalabya* to offer to the fearful;
and now imagine how, at the end of a summer far from Lebanon,
the migrant cucumber, seeking only nourishment and the touch of bees,
sends out one flower of defiant yellow, and soon, new fruit.

Stone of Return

for Greg Lehman

A drop of spittle
falls on the red stone
he holds in his palm, flares
and sinks to a darker stain. He pivots
a forefinger on the wet place
then reaches for my hands,
turning each one over
to where it's whitest, at the wrist,
and smears a line like a bridge
across the broken river of my veins.
                    Now that this country
has been all but emptied of his people's hands
by cordons of fire and poisoned flour,
and its tongues have retreated
to hang in the eucalypts and curl the breakers
that boom under granite like cannon-fire,
who will tell how to live out here, who
make sense of a bed of scattered bones?
                    You might say
this piece of ochre found a man
who, kneeling in the mirror-worked saltmarsh
that levels the edge of the bay,
would know it at once, practise its ancient
red alchemy of give and receive,
and pass it from hand to hand.

Notes and Attributions

p.16 Range Light
Range Lights help mariners find the channel once they are in a harbour.
These lighthouses come in pairs, the front range being at a lower
elevation than the back range. A mariner sails until they are in line, one
above the other, indicating that the vessel is in the channel.

The final lines of this poem echo lines from John Burnside's poem
'Haar': 'a dream I can't forget/ and never quite recall.'

p.33 On Solitude
Passages in italics are quotations from the sources below:

> Rousseau, J-J. 1979 *Meditations of a Solitary Walker* (selections
> from *Reveries of the Solitary Walker*), Harmondsworth:
> Penguin.

> Nietzsche, F. 1996 *Zarathustra* (selections from *Thus Spake
> Zarathustra,* 1899) London: Phoenix

> Emerson, RW. 2008 *Nature* (selections from Nature and
> Selected Essays) London: Penguin

p.35 Blue Halo
Barbara Blackman became blind in her early twenties. She is reported
to have said: 'One's life has many autobiographies. It depends on where
you place a shaft of memory'; 'I wasn't born with a silver spoon in my
mouth but with… a question mark'; 'I float in the present, seemingly
held up by many hands.'

p.40 When she thinks of Robert Hass's aspens
Hass's lines are: 'There are limits to saying,/ in language, what the tree did.' from 'The Problem of Describing Trees'.

p.56 Thistle Villanelle
This poem's refrain owes a debt to a series of prints and paintings by Joan Ross entitled *Imagine if they'd cared,* 'that ask us to imagine a world where colonial settlers had cared about the environment.' *nsmithgallery.com*

p.59 How to treat a dairy cow
Emerald is a real cow, rescued from an industrial-scale dairy and nursed back to health by Emma Haswell and her team at Brightside Farm Sanctuary. The poem paraphrases a line from Stephen Dobyns' 'Spiritual Chickens': 'squeezed/ between the world and his idea of the world'.